W9-CMK-904

PLEASE WASH
YOUR HANDS
BEFORE YOU READ ME
AND KEEP ME CLEAN

My World

My
Continent

by Heather Adamson

Consulting Editor: Gail Saunders-Smith, PhD
Consultant: Susan B. Neuman, EdD
Former U.S. Assistant Secretary for Elementary
and Secondary Education
Professor, Educational Studies, University of Michigan

Capstone
press
Mankato, Minnesota

Pebble Books are published by Capstone Press,
151 Good Counsel Drive, P.O. Box 669, Mankato, Minnesota 56002.
www.capstonepress.com

1 2 3 4 5 6 10 09 08 07 06 05

Library of Congress Cataloging-in-Publication Data
Adamson, Heather, 1974–
    My continent / by Heather Adamson.
    p. cm.—(Pebble Books. My world)
    Summary: "Simple text and photographs introduce basic community concepts
related to continents including location, things on a continent, and differences
between continents"—Provided by publisher.
    Includes bibliographical references and index.
    ISBN 0-7368-4235-7 (hardcover)
    1. Geography—Juvenile literature. 2. Continents—Juvenile literature. I. Title.
II. Series: My world (Mankato, Minn.)
G133.A329 2006
910'.914'1—dc22   2004030960

Note to Parents and Teachers

The My World set supports social studies standards related to
community. This book describes and illustrates basic community
concepts related to continents. The images support early readers in
understanding the text. The repetition of words and phrases helps
early readers learn new words. This book also introduces early
readers to subject-specific vocabulary words, which are defined in
the Glossary section. Early readers may need assistance to read
some words and to use the Table of Contents, Glossary, Read More,
Internet Sites, and Index sections of the book.

Table of Contents

My Continent

My continent is
North America.
A continent is
a large area of land.

North America

Pacific
Ocean

Atlantic
Ocean

N
W—E
S

Oceans are
around continents.
The Pacific Ocean
is west of my continent.
The Atlantic Ocean
is east of my continent.

North America

Greenland

Canada

United States

Mexico

Places on My Continent

Continents have countries.
Canada, the United States,
and Mexico are part
of my continent.

People live
in many places
on my continent.
Some people live
near mountains.

My friend lives in Mexico.
Her home is by the ocean.

Other Continents

Earth has seven continents. They are North America, South America, Africa, Antarctica, Asia, Australia, and Europe.

Continents have different weather. Africa is hot.

Antarctica is cold.

North America
can be warm and cold.

People live on
almost every continent.
What have you learned
about your continent?

Glossary

Africa—the second-largest continent; Africa is south of Europe between the Atlantic and Indian Oceans.

Antarctica—a continent on the very southern part of Earth

Canada—a country in northern North America

continent—one of the seven main land areas of Earth

country—a part of land where people live and have a government

Mexico—a country in southern North America

North America—the third-largest continent; North America is between the Pacific Ocean and the Atlantic Ocean.

ocean—a large body of salt water

Read More

Bagley, Katie. *North America.* Continents. Mankato, Minn.: Bridgestone Books, 2003.

Nelson, Robin. *Where is My Continent?* Where am I? Minneapolis: Lerner, 2002.

Waters, Jennifer. *The Continents.* Spyglass Books. Minneapolis: Compass Point Books, 2003.

Internet Sites

FactHound offers a safe, fun way to find Internet sites related to this book. All of the sites on FactHound have been researched by our staff.

Here's how:

1. Visit *www.facthound.com*
2. Type in this special code **0736842357** for age-appropriate sites. Or enter a search word related to this book for a more general search.
3. Click on the **Fetch It** button.

FactHound will fetch the best sites for you!

Index

Word Count: 117
Grade: 1
Early-Intervention Level: 12

Editorial Credits
Mari C. Schuh, editor; Juliette Peters, designer and illustrator; Jo Miller, photo researcher; Scott Thoms, photo editor

Photo Credits
Art Directors/A. Gasson, 18
Bruce Coleman Inc./Joe McDonald, 16
Capstone Press/Karon Dubke, cover (foreground), 1, (foreground), 4, (foreground), 20 (foreground)
Cheryl R. Richter, 4 (background), 20 (background)
Corbis/James Marshall, 12; Photo Library International, 6
Unicorn Stock Photos/Mark E. Gibson, 1 (background), 14